LET'S VISIT THE WEST INDIES

Let's visit the
WEST INDIES

JOHN C. CALDWELL

BURKE

ACKNOWLEDGEMENTS

The publishers are grateful to Anne Bolt for permission to reproduce the colour illustrations
in this edition and to the following for permission to reproduce the black-and-white illustrations:

B.W.I.A.; Barbados Tourist Board; Jamaica Tourist Board; Martinique Tourist
Board; Netherlands West Indies Tourist Board; Office du Tourisme, Martinique;
V.E.B. Nicholson.

The cover photograph of a sugar-cane cutter is reproduced by permission of Tate and Lyle
Refineries Ltd.

Burke Publishing Company Limited,
14 John Street, London, WC1N 2EJ.
Burke Publishing (Canada) Limited,
73 Six Point Road, Toronto 18, Ontario.
Made and printed by offset in Great Britain by
William Clowes & Sons, Limited, London, Beccles and Colchester

Contents

BAHAMA

ISLANDS

C U B A

Caicos
Islands
(Part of Ja

Tu
Islo

Manzanillo
Santiago de Cuba

Windward Passage

Little Cayman
Cayman
Brac
Grand Cayman
(Part of Jamaica)

HAITI
DOMINI

Port-au-Prince

Montego Bay
JAMAICA
Kingston
(H I S P A N

LEEWARD
ISLANDS

Anguilla
Saint Martin (Fr. West Indies)
Sint Maarten (Neth. West Indies)
St. Barthélemy (Fr. West Indies)
Saba (Neth. West Indies)
Sint Eustatius
(Neth. West Indies)
St. Kitts
Basseterre
Nevis
Montserrat

Barbuda
(Part of Antigua)

St. John's
Antigua

Guadeloupe
Passage
Pointe-à-pitre
Guadeloupe
(French West Indies)
Basse Terre

Marie Galante (Fr.
West Indies)
Dominica

Miles   50
0
0   50
Kilometres

WINDWARD
ISLANDS

Portsmouth
Dominica
Roseau

Martinique Passage

Sainte Marie
Fort-de-   Martinique
France   Lamentin
(French West Indies)

Castries   St. Lucia

St. Vincent Passage
St. Vincent

Barbados
Bridgetown

Bequia

The
Grenadines
(Part of Grenada)

Grenada
St. George's

Miles   50
0
0   50
Kilometres

Don Pitcher

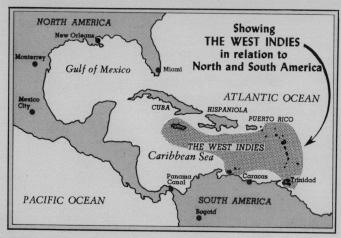

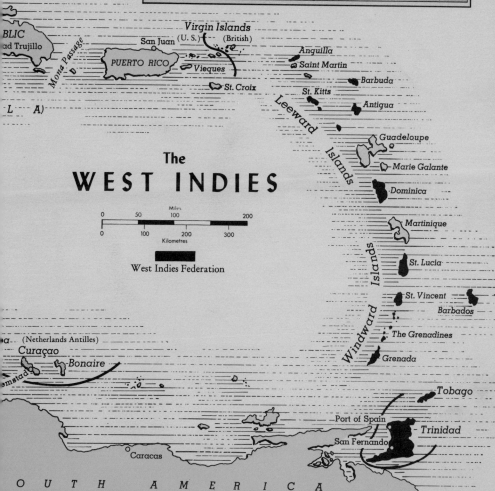

One of the many beautiful beaches for which Jamaica is famous

Let's Visit the West Indies

The West Indies are a string of islands stretching in a rough arc from Florida in North America and Yucatan in Central America to Venezuela in South America. Let's look at the map so that we may know the location of all the important islands, and especially of those we will visit in this book. The many islands may be divided into three groups: the Bahama Islands, the Greater Antilles and the Lesser Antilles.

First, the Bahamas consist of twenty inhabited and as many as seven hundred uninhabited islands in the Atlantic Ocean. This group of islands, belonging to Great Britain, is within 50 miles (80 kilometres) of the Florida coast of the United States.

South and south-east of Florida, between the Atlantic Ocean and the Caribbean Sea, lie several large islands called the Greater Antilles. Cuba, the nearest of these to the United States, is the largest island in the Caribbean. To the east of Cuba is the second largest island, Hispaniola, which is divided into two countries named Haiti and the Dominican Republic. Next to Hispaniola is Puerto Rico, which is a possession of the United States. Jamaica, which comes next in size to Hispaniola, lies south-east of Cuba, and is the largest island in what is still known as the British West Indies. ("British" is used to describe those islands in the West Indies which were originally colonised by the British, although some of them have now become independent members of the Commonwealth.)

9

Looking east and south of these big islands, we see the many smaller ones which stretch down to the coast of South America. These islands are known as the Lesser Antilles. They also lie between the Caribbean Sea and the Atlantic Ocean.

Sometimes all three groups of islands are called the West Indies. However, in recent years this term has been used to refer to the "British" islands of both the Greater and the Lesser Antilles and the French and Dutch islands of the latter.

It would be difficult to visit all of the many islands in one book. Therefore in this book we shall learn about the French West Indies and the Dutch West Indies. We will learn, also, as much as we can about the British West Indies, of which three territories, Trinidad and Tobago, Jamaica and Barbados, are now completely independent.

For a few years, from 1958 when Princess Margaret opened the new Parliament of the West Indies, these islands were united to form the West Indies Federation. But the newly-born state died when first Jamaica and then Trinidad decided to withdraw and to become individually independent countries. Other islands have varying degrees of self-government.

Sugar is the main product of most of the islands; but Jamaica also has bauxite (aluminium ore); Trinidad produces oil and from its famous pitch lake comes the world's largest supply of natural asphalt. St. Vincent grows arrowroot and Grenada is the island of nutmegs. The islands also produce coconuts, bananas and most other tropical fruit,

10

which are shipped regularly to Britain and other countries.

The islands of the West Indies have all, at one time or another, belonged to European nations. As we study the history of the islands, we will learn of the wars fought for their possession, as well as of the buccaneers and pirates who once upon a time had their headquarters in the West Indies.

During the Caribbean wars, islands changed ownership a dozen or even fourteen times. When peace finally came to the area, ownership of islands was very mixed. We find the two main islands of the French West Indies separated by islands which were British possessions. We will visit one little island, covering only 37 square miles (96 square kilometres), which is divided between France and Holland; yet everyone there speaks English.

But before we learn about the wars which caused the islands to change hands so often, let's read about the geography and climate of the West Indies.

An aerial view of sugar-cane fields on Barbados, one of the older islands of the West Indies

Geography and Climate

Millions of years ago a mountain range extended across the Caribbean and along the edge of the Atlantic Ocean. Geologists have named this the Caribbean Andes. The islands of the Caribbean are really mountain-tops. There are also many volcanoes, mostly extinct but a few still active. Most of the islands are volcanic.

Let's take another look at the map to discover some further facts. Can you find Antigua and Barbados? These islands are actually in the Atlantic Ocean rather than the Caribbean Sea. Antigua, Barbados and several smaller islands might be called the "outer islands". There are no high mountains on these. Geologists tell us that they are older islands, having been above the sea for a longer time.

The "inner" or "younger" island chain includes St. Kitts, the French islands of Guadeloupe and Martinique, Dominica, St. Lucia, Grenada and many small islets. The mountains on the younger islands are high; there are volcanoes, both extinct and active. The soil and vegetation differ somewhat from those of the low-lying outer islands.

There is still volcanic action on several islands. One of the most destructive eruptions in history took place on Martinique in 1902. Mt. Pelée, a 4,700-foot (1,431-metre) volcano, erupted and destroyed St. Pierre, then the capital city. More than 30,000 people were killed.

The West Indies are famous for beautiful beaches. Except

The inner islands are very mountainous. This picture shows a typical mountain area

in areas near volcanoes, where the sand is black, the beaches are of fine, white sand. If one were to fly over these lovely beaches, the water would seem to be of several colours. This is because of the coral reefs that lie offshore. Coral is of different colours, and this makes the water appear to be different shades of blue, green, yellow or red.

Now let's look at our map once again and locate the large island named Trinidad. It is the southernmost island in the West Indies and is very close to South America. It is so close —7 miles (11·2 kilometres) at the narrowest point—that one can easily see the mountains of Venezuela from it. Trinidad and other small islands near South America were once part of that continent.

Millions of years ago, Trinidad became separated from the mainland. However, soil, trees and flowers, birds and animals are still similar to those found in nearby Venezuela. We say that, geologically, Trinidad is part of South America.

All of the West Indies are within the part of the world

which we call the tropics. We know that tropical countries are usually hot and that they often have heavy rainfall. However, the climate of the West Indies is not very hot, nor is the rainfall all that heavy.

There is, of course, no winter or summer as we know them, although there are variations in temperature, and in rainfall and humidity levels.

The average low temperature is approximately 25° Centigrade (76° Fahrenheit). During the hottest season the average may be as high as 29° Centigrade (85° Fahrenheit).

There is much less rain than we would expect for the tropics. In fact, several islands have a water problem. There is not enough rain to keep streams flowing. While most of the rain falls during recognised wetter months, there is no heavy rainy season such as occurs in other parts of the tropics.

West Indians are proud of their weather. Even during the

hottest season, the climate is pleasant because of what are called the trade winds. There is always a pleasant breeze.

The combination of an unusually good climate and beautiful beaches is very important to the people of the West Indies since it attracts many tourists. The money spent by visitors is enough to make tourism the largest business on several islands. Most of the people who spend their holidays there are Americans and Canadians, who visit the West Indies only during their winter months. West Indians hope that people will learn that the weather is fine all year round. Then more tourists will come all through the year.

It is because of the constant presence of the trade winds that the islands are divided into two groups. These winds blow from the north-east. The northernmost islands are more sheltered from the trade winds and are called the Leeward Islands. The southern islands of the Lesser Antilles are less protected and are known as the Windward Islands. The

Montego Bay, a famous tourist attraction. Note the offshore reef

Atlantic or eastern side of each island is always called the Windward coast, while the more sheltered western side is known as the Leeward coast.

Now we know about temperature, wind and rainfall. What varieties of trees and other vegetation are found on the islands? We would expect to find palms and beautiful tropical flowers on islands within the tropics. And there certainly are coconut-palms, and many tropical flowers and crops, on every island. However, a strange fact about the West Indies is that many of the beautiful flowers, the best-known trees, even the most important crops, came from faraway lands.

For instance, the breadfruit tree which is found on several of the islands and which provides food for many people was brought to the West Indies from the South Pacific by a famous Englishman named Captain Bligh. Bligh also brought

Breadfruit trees grow wild on almost all the islands. The fruit has become a favourite food in the West Indies

bananas and the coconut-palm to several islands. He commanded the ship *Bounty* whose crew mutinied during a voyage in the South Pacific. A famous book, later made into a film, was written about the mutiny on the *Bounty*.

Coffee came to the West Indies from South America, the cocoa tree from the South Pacific. The mango, an important fruit, came from India. The first Spanish settlers brought citrus fruits and sugar-cane, which became the most important crop. And because of sugar-cane, the most common animal is also an import from India. The owners of cane plantations found that rats destroyed much of their crop. Then someone had the idea of bringing the mongoose from India. This little animal, which looks like a large ferret, kills rats, snakes and many varieties of birds which nest in the ground. Because of the large number of mongooses there are few snakes left, and poisonous snakes are found only on one island. Unfortunately, however, this fierce little animal has a big appetite and likes to raid chicken coops! Now there are so many mongooses on some islands that people are wondering how to control their number.

There are many other trees and flowers that came from far away: the hibiscus from China, spices from the East Indies, the beautiful bougainvillaea from South America. As we learn about the history of the West Indies, we will discover how these flowers, trees and crops arrived. We will learn also how the original inhabitants disappeared, and how their place was taken by people from three continents. These many

changes began when Christopher Columbus discovered the
West Indies in 1492 and visited them again in 1493 and subse-
quent years.

The Arrival of Columbus

The West Indies and North America were discovered by
Europeans racing each other to find the spices of South-east
Asia. As an outcome, colonists came to the Western Hemisphere and new countries were born. It began during the
fifteenth century when Spain and Portugal were the great
seafaring nations of Europe; but the discovery of the Western
Hemisphere was really accidental.

During the fifteenth century, a few spices such as pepper,
nutmeg, cloves and cinnamon began to reach Europe. The
people of Europe were excited by these flavourings which
could make food more tasty. It was known that the spices
came from islands off the coast of South-east Asia, or from
the mainland of Asia.

Trying to find the Spice Islands, the Portuguese sailed
southward, round the tip of Africa, and then into the Indian
Ocean. The Spaniards, led by Christopher Columbus, sailed
westward across the Atlantic Ocean. The race was close. In
1499, Vasco da Gama reached the coast of India and picked
up a cargo of spices. Columbus had reached the West Indies
a few years earlier. In 1513, the first Portuguese ship reached
the Molucca Islands where most of the spices grew. In that

18

Caribs building
a dugout canoe
on the stormy
Windward coast.
This scene must
be much as it
was in
Columbus' time

same year, Balboa crossed the Isthmus of Panama and discovered the Pacific Ocean.

Although the race was close, the Portuguese were the winners, for they reached the real Spice Islands. Columbus and the other Spaniards who followed him discovered a new world but no spices.

Do you remember this little rhyme?

In 1492 Columbus sailed the ocean blue;
In 1493 he sailed the deep blue sea.

All the important islands of the West Indies were discovered by Columbus during his four voyages which began in 1492 and continued until 1503. In some cases, we know the exact day when the lookout on Columbus' flag ship shouted, "Land ho!" In other cases, we know the month, or sometimes only the year.

Jamaica was discovered on May 4th, 1494. Dominica,

19

Martinique and Guadeloupe were reached a few months earlier, in 1493. Trinidad, Tobago, Grenada and St. Vincent were discovered in 1498. St. Lucia was discovered on Columbus' fourth voyage in 1502, and the Cayman Islands were reached in 1503.

Columbus named most of the islands. Sometimes he used the name of the Catholic saint on whose day he reached an island. At other times, he used a name descriptive of the island. When he reached Trinidad, his ships anchored in sight of three hills, and he chose the name La Trinidad, which is Spanish for "the trinity", or a group of three.

Many of the islands were inhabited by Indians when the Spanish ships arrived. There were two Indian tribes living in the Caribbean, the Arawaks and the Caribs. The Arawaks, peaceful farmers and fishermen, were the first Indians Columbus saw. This tribe thought that the strange white men, dressed in armour, were gods. They provided Columbus' men with food and water.

We know more about Columbus' visits to Jamaica than elsewhere. On his second visit to that island there was trouble with the usually peaceful Arawaks. The Spanish sailors treated the Indians cruelly, and the Arawaks refused to provide any more food. This led to fights in which many Arawaks were killed.

It is estimated that there were 60,000 Arawaks living in Jamaica. There were many Indians of this tribe living on other islands also: but either because of ill-treatment, or

20

because of disease brought by the Spaniards, the Arawaks died out completely within a short time. Today there are no Arawaks, only a few traces left here and there of a once large tribe.

The second Indian tribe, the Caribs, gave their name to the Caribbean. These Indians were fierce and determined fighters. They often fought the peaceful Arawaks, driving them from islands or making them into slaves. Sometimes the Caribs were friendly when Columbus' men went ashore. At other times, often because of Spanish cruelty, the Caribs fought the strange white men.

Other Spanish ships followed Columbus. As more Europeans arrived in the West Indies, the Caribs became more unfriendly. On some islands they were quickly defeated. On others they continued to fight. They kept Europeans from settling on Dominica for two hundred years. And on St. Vincent the Caribs fought European invasion for almost three hundred years. Thousands of Caribs were killed, others died of disease, were enslaved or deported to South America. Now there are only a few hundred left.

Most of the remaining Caribs live on a reservation in Dominica, one of the smaller British islands. The Caribs did not stop fighting until quite recently. In 1930 the last Carib "war" took place in Dominica when the Indians rose against police who, they believed, were ill-treating them.

Great changes took place in the West Indies after Columbus discovered the islands. Now, all of the tens of thousands of

Few pure-blooded Caribs remain in the West Indies. Among them are this father and son, seen here operating a primitive sugar-press

Arawak Indians who once lived on the islands are gone. Only a few hundred of the once fierce and proud Carib tribe remain. And, as we shall learn, the place of the Indians was soon taken by people of other races from far away.

It is said that Columbus believed until he died that the islands he discovered were off the coast of India. That is why he called the Arawaks and Caribs "Indians". He continued to search for the spices, the silver and gold he was sure could be found, as did other explorers who followed him.

Columbus claimed the first islands for Spain, and Spanish settlers began to arrive on several of them. It was they who brought citrus fruits from Spain; they who introduced the sugar-cane which became the most important crop in the West Indies.

It was not long before other Europeans followed the Spaniards: English, French and Dutch explorers and colonists. For three hundred years the European nations fought for control of the West Indies, for the islands became valuable when it was found that sugar-cane grew well. And when thousands of African slaves were brought to work the great sugar plantations or estates, the discoveries of Columbus became even more valuable.

Now we will read about the island wars and some of the famous men who took part in the struggle for the West Indies.

The Caribbean Wars

The history of the West Indies is closely related to that of both North America and South America. There were many fine harbours in the West Indies which became provisioning ports for explorers of both continents. We have mentioned that in 1513 Balboa reached Panama and first saw the Pacific Ocean. In the same year, Ponce de Leon reached Florida. In 1519, Hernando Cortes began the conquest of Mexico. In 1541, Hernando de Soto discovered the Mississippi River; in 1565, the city of St. Augustine, Florida, was founded by the Spaniards.

We can see from this that, for many years after Columbus' voyages, the Spaniards continued to be the great explorers of the New World. Spanish admirals and *conquistadors* claimed and conquered the West Indies, Mexico and parts of South America. It is interesting to know that Jamaica, the third largest Caribbean island, was given to Columbus' family by the

The row of cannon is a silent reminder that this old fort once had to be hotly defended

king and queen of Spain. It is strange, therefore, that in spite of Spanish explorations and settlements, no Spanish colonies in the Western Hemisphere remain today, and that there are only three islands in the Caribbean where Spanish is spoken.

Spain was able to hold Mexico only until 1822, parts of South America until 1824, Cuba and Puerto Rico until 1898, the Dominican Republic until 1821. Although Spain gave its language, and the Catholic religion, to much of the New World, the Spanish were poor colonists.

In 1588, a great sea battle took place which changed Spanish fortunes. In that year the Spanish Armada attempted to conquer England. This great fleet was defeated and most of its ships were sunk, an event that marked the beginning of Spain's decline.

After the Spanish defeat, more and more English ships appeared in the New World. In 1595, Sir Walter Raleigh visited the West Indies, searching for Eldorado—a land of great riches that was supposed to be somewhere in the Western Hemisphere. We will read later about the discovery he made on the island of Trinidad.

Soon French and Dutch ships were also sailing across the Atlantic. New York and the Hudson River Valley were explored and settled by the Dutch.

Peter Stuyvesant, first governor of Nieuw Amsterdam (the city which we now call New York), was among the best known of the Dutchmen who explored and fought for West Indian islands. In fact, he lost a leg while leading an expedition to recapture the tiny island of St. Martin, claimed by Holland in 1631 but conquered by the French a few years later. In 1648, the French and Dutch decided to divide the small island peacefully. They each chose one of their leading citizens. The two men stood back to back, and then started walking around the island in opposite directions. The territory covered by each man then became the territory of his country. As the island has an area of only 37 square miles (96 square kilometres), the walk was not too long! The French part is called St. Martin, the Dutch section Sint Maarten.

But the ownership of the other islands was not settled in such a peaceful manner. The worst battles took place between the French and English. Dominica changed hands fifteen times. St. Lucia, which was originally claimed by France, and then fought over, changed ownership fourteen times. Today a French patois is still the most commonly spoken language in St. Lucia.

Before learning how the ownership of islands was finally decided, let's read about other battles fought by the "brethren of the coast". This was the name given to the pirates, buccaneers and privateers who sailed the Caribbean. (Privateer was also the name given to an armed ship, privately owned, which had government permission to capture ships of an enemy nation.) Many men became rich by being privateers because the captains and crews could keep much of the cargo of captured ships. Buccaneers did the same thing without any government permission.

One of
St. Lucia's
beautiful bays

For many years privateers and buccaneers preyed on Spanish ships which were taking treasure from Mexico and South America to Spain. Captain Henry Morgan, who made his headquarters at Port Royal, Jamaica, was among the most famous buccaneers. Morgan and his men captured scores of Spanish galleons filled with gold and silver. They even attacked cities in Central America (which was then called the Spanish Main). They looted cities, and took the citizens as hostages. In the middle of the seventeenth century, Port Royal, Jamaica, was described as "the richest and wickedest city on earth".

The British government made peace with Henry Morgan, and he was made Lieutenant-Governor of Jamaica; whereupon he began to make war on his old comrades. Then, on June 7th, 1692, there was a great earthquake in Jamaica. Port Royal was destroyed as most of the city slid into the

27

sea. It is thought that great riches went into the sea with it; and as recently as 1959 and 1960 an expedition of trained divers tried to recover some of the treasure. It is also thought that there may be buried treasure on several other islands.

Many of the battles between the French and British took place during the American Revolution. The French were allied with the American colonists. The British used the West Indies as a base from which their ships sailed to intercept French ships trying to supply the colonists.

English Harbour in Antigua became one of England's most important naval bases. Admiral Lord Nelson, while still Captain Nelson, built shipyards there. Admiral Rodney was another famous Englishman whose ships sailed from English Harbour and, in April, 1782, defeated the French fleet in the Battle of the Saints.

Within twenty years the French were back—this time allied with the Spaniards. A combined French and Spanish fleet sailed into the Caribbean, but Nelson led his fleet from English Harbour and chased the French and Spaniards all the way across the Atlantic. On October 26th, 1805, the French and Spaniards were defeated at the Battle of Trafalgar, in which Lord Nelson lost his life.

The ownership of most of the islands was settled by 1805, but Guadeloupe did not become a permanent French possession until 1816. And, in 1877, the French bought St. Barthelemy, or St. Barts as it is called, from Sweden.

Because of the years of fighting, there are many interesting old forts all through the West Indies. We have mentioned English Harbour and Nelson's Dockyard in Antigua. Every island has at least one ancient fortress. No one knows how many ships lie sunk along the coast of the islands, but eighty-three have been located around the shores of one small island named Barbuda.

On the following page there is a chart which lists the important islands, showing which belong to the British West Indies, to the French West Indies and to the Netherlands West Indies. But before we visit the islands to learn about the people and how they live there now, a little more should be said about the islands' history.

We have learned that the Spaniards introduced sugar-cane to Jamaica. This became a major crop on every island, and the establishment of big sugar plantations had many important effects on the life of the islands. When the Indians died out, or were killed, it was necessary to find workers for the sugar-cane fields. It was during the many years when sugar was king that new people were brought to the West Indies, first from Africa and later from India, China and Madeira.

Lord Nelson's name is closely associated with Antigua

THE WEST INDIES

Name	Population	Location
British West Indies		
1. Jamaica	1,800,000	90 miles (145 kms) south of Cuba
Cayman Islands	9,000	178 miles (286 kms) north-west of Jamaica
Turks and Caicos Islands	6,700	450 miles (724 kms) north-west of Jamaica
2. British Virgin Islands	8,600	Adjoining U.S. Virgin Islands; south-east of Puerto Rico and north-west of the most northerly Leeward island St. Kitts
3. British Leeward Islands	147,000	The Leeward Islands begin 150 miles (241 kms) south-east of Puerto Rico
Antigua		
Anguilla		
St. Kitts		
Nevis		
Montserrat		
Barbuda		
4. British Windward Islands	350,000	The Windward Islands are situated directly south of the Leeward Islands
Grenada and the Grena-dines		
St. Lucia		
St. Vincent		
Dominica		
5. Barbados	240,000	100 miles (161 kms) east of St. Vincent (in the Atlantic Ocean)
6. Trinidad and Tobago	970,000	9 miles (14 kms) east of Venezuela (most southerly of West Indies)
French West Indies		
1. Martinique	300,000	Between Dominica and St. Lucia in the Windward Islands
2. Guadeloupe and nearby islands	300,000	Largest and most southerly of the Leeward Islands
3. St. Martin and St. Barts	7,000	Near the northern end of the Leeward Islands
Netherlands West Indies		
1. Leeward Group		
Aruba	60,000	15 to 75 miles (24 to 121 kms) north of the coast of Venezuela
Bonaire	6,000	
Curaçao	132,000	
2. Windward Group		The Netherlands Windward Islands are actually near the northern end of the Leeward Islands, 175 miles (281 kms) south-east of Puerto Rico
Sint Maarten	3,700	
Saba	1,100	
St. Eustatius	1,150	

30

When Sugar Was King

The Spaniards found that the Arawak Indians were not good farm workers. These Indians were not accustomed to heavy work, day after day, and those who did not escape soon died. As we have already learned, the Arawaks disappeared completely soon after the discovery of the West Indies.

The Spaniards and, later, other Europeans solved this problem in the same way as a similar problem was solved by the plantation owners in the American colonies. At the same time as the New World was being opened up, Europeans were exploring the coast of West Africa. Many European ship-owners were soon engaged in the capturing of Africans for sale as slaves. When the sugar estates were established in the West Indies, and big plantations were started in the American colonies, slavery became big business. Tens of thousands of African slaves were brought to the West Indies. Many men became rich as slave traders.

We can understand the importance of slavery by reading about Barbados. This island is the most easterly of the West

Today sugar is loaded mechanically, as in this picture

Indies and was settled by the British in 1624. It is the only island of the West Indies that never changed hands—it remained British until achieving full independence in November, 1966.

The first settlers tried to farm by using white workers, known as "redlegs". These men were political prisoners or religious dissenters. This means that they had rebelled against the established religion or political régime of England, and because of this had been deported. However, the estate owners of Barbados found that the redlegs were not suitable for the work, and they then began to buy African slaves.

By 1685 there were 46,000 Negro slaves on Barbados. Thousands of slaves were brought to the other islands also. Wherever sugar was grown, the population became mostly Negro. Sugar became king of all the crops. All but the most mountainous areas of every island were cleared and planted with sugar-cane, and vast quantities of sugar and molasses were produced each year. Rum was also made from sugar, and is still an important product in several islands.

Some sugar estates covered huge areas and required the labour of hundreds of slaves. Each estate had a Great House where the owner lived, with the slave quarters located around it. Some of the old Great Houses are now in ruins, others are still in good repair. One of the most famous of these Great Houses, Rose Hall, is supposed to be haunted. It was owned by a cruel woman who murdered several husbands and killed many slaves. The slaves finally rebelled against

The haunted ruins of Rose Hall, Jamaica

ill-treatment and murdered their owner; it is the ghost of the murdered woman who is supposed to haunt Rose Hall now.

Sugar was king for almost two centuries. Other crops were grown, but none was as important as sugar. The life of the people was dependent upon this crop. If the price of sugar was low, the estate owners, shipowners and merchants all suffered. And in 1834 something happened in England that ruined many estate owners and changed the lives of many West Indians.

People in England and other European countries were becoming aware of the wrongs of the slave trade, and in 1834 slavery was made illegal throughout the British Empire.

33

Sugar, which in some colonies had made people rich, now helped to make the same people paupers; for although some of the freed slaves were willing to work on the estates, many others refused to do the hard work. They preferred, instead, to become small independent farmers. Some estate owners tried to keep going with a few workers; others even tried to handle the crops by themselves. But all farm work was done by hand in the 1800s, and when an estate owner's "hands" were taken away, it was almost impossible to stay in business.

In time, machinery came into use; and, in addition, numerous freed Negroes decided that working in the cane fields wasn't so bad after all. But it was too late for many ruined owners.

On a few islands the problem of workers was solved in an interesting way. In about 1860, the British government persuaded a number of farmers from India to come to Trinidad as independent workers. India was a British colony with a population of 300,000,000 people. Many Indians were willing to leave their homes to work in the West Indies for a certain number of years in return for their passage there and back.

By 1870, there were 28,000 Indians living in Trinidad. By

This girl, like many of the people in the West Indies, is descended from Africans who were brought over as slaves to work in the sugar plantations

1883, their numbers had increased to 48,000. The Indians liked the West Indies. The climate was better than that of their homeland. They could make more money. When their terms of service were completed, many of the Indians remained, having saved enough money to send home for their families.

Today there are over 300,000 Indians in Trinidad, more than 30,000 in Jamaica, and several thousand more living on smaller islands. Many of these Indians dress and live as they would in their homeland. Some are Hindus, some Moslems. They have brought Indian crops, fruits and trees to the islands. Many of these early workers came from parts of India where rice was cultivated. Their descendants grow rice on Trinidad, even using the big water-buffaloes that are common as plough animals in many parts of Asia where rice is an important crop.

We have already read that the mongoose, the most common animal on many islands, is a native of India. The Indians also brought the mango trees whose fruit has become important on all the larger islands. Sometimes called the king of tropical fruits, the mango is now very plentiful in the West Indies.

The Hindus and Moslems from India are called East Indians so that they will not be confused with the few "American Indians" still living in the West Indies.

They all came because of sugar. We can see now how important sugar has been to the West Indies. Because of

A farmer from the Jamaican mountains. Note the rather unusual form of saddle-bag

sugar, tens of thousands of slaves were brought from Africa—which has resulted in most of the population being Negro. Then, when slavery was abolished, thousands of Hindus and Moslems came from India. The Indians brought rice, as well as water-buffaloes, the mongoose and the islands' most popular fruit.

In the course of time, with the help of the Indians, with the use of machinery, and with better working conditions, sugar again became the foremost West Indian crop.

Sugar, molasses and rum are still the most important products; but new crops have also become important. And in the West Indies today there are other races in addition to the Indians and Negroes; amongst them are many Chinese and Portuguese (from Madeira) who were also brought in as labourers. Trinidad, in particular, has a wonderful mixture of races.

The Chinese in the West Indies have become very good businessmen, operating in many spheres, including hotels, restaurants and laundries. In Jamaica, there is a saying: "All grocery shops are owned by Chinese; all drapers' shops by Lebanese and Syrians". This is because the West Indies have become a melting pot of many races. Immigrants have come from Asia, Europe and the Middle East. Many of the most successful businessmen have come from Lebanon or Syria. One of the West Indies' richest men was once an immigrant pedlar, selling odds and ends to Negro farmers. Now this man owns half a dozen businesses.

Each of these air hostesses is of a different origin, though they are all West Indian

The West Indies are fortunate in the fact that island slavery was ended without war, and racial problems have solved themselves with few resentments. In the West Indies, there is no segregation of races. White, Negro, Chinese and Indian children go to the same schools.

Everyone speaks the language of the country of which they are citizens: so that Negroes in the French islands speak French; those who live in the Netherlands West Indies speak Dutch. English is the most widely spoken language because there are more "British" islands than others; also many residents of Dutch and French islands speak English. As we shall learn as we visit the islands, there are sometimes dialects or special ways of speaking in which words from several languages are used.

Some people in the West Indies feel it is unfortunate that the islands must be separated, not only by the ocean but by allegiance and language as well. They dream of a time when *all* the islands may become federated as part of one island nation with no "British", "Dutch" or "French" tag to keep them apart. To them it was a considerable disappointment when the Federation of what had been the British West Indies fell apart, for this had been the basis on which they had hoped to build.

Our first visit will be to the islands that went to make up the Federation, but which are now separate entities again. The chart on page 30 gives the population of each of the main islands, and its location in the Caribbean. By studying the chart and the map, it will be possible to locate all the islands of the British West Indies, and to understand their location in relation to other islands.

The "British" West Indies

In 1958, the British government offered independence to its colonies in the Caribbean. A group of twenty-seven small islands called the British Virgin Islands decided that they did not want independence. They are located close to Puerto Rico and the American Virgin Islands. Almost all business is with neighbouring American possessions. Even American money is used. Two British colonies on the mainland— British Guiana (now the independent Guyana) in South America and British Honduras in Central America—which are not strictly part of the West Indies, were also invited to join the Federation but declined.

However, all the other colonies of Great Britain, consisting of thirteen islands and scores of islets, decided to join the new West Indies Federation. The new Federation had its first national elections in 1958. It was scheduled to become completely independent in 1962. Unfortunately it lasted only until 1961, when Mr. Norman Manley, the Prime Minister, was defeated in an election by his cousin, Sir Alexander

Bustamante, who was against the idea of the West Indies Federation. The people of Jamaica voted 251,935 to 216,000 to withdraw from the Federation and to form their own independent government.

If we look at the map of the West Indies we can understand some of the problems that faced the West Indies Federation. If we draw a line from Jamaica to the Turks and Caicos Islands, which were dependencies of Jamaica, thence to the other members of the Federation, the distance is 1,600 miles (2,574 kilometres). This line passes over the territory of six other nations.

Although the islands are all well served by air, through British West Indian Airways' daily services, the long distances between islands, and the general transportation problems, were among the difficulties faced by the new Federation. As

Until recently, many of the islands could only be reached by small boats like this one

Almost all the islands now have their own air services. The initials on this plane waiting at St. Vincent Airport stand for Leeward Islands Air Transport

a result of the distances between island and island the people remained to a large extent strangers to each other; they did not really support the Federation to which so much lip-service had been paid. Then there were the problems involved in making the Federation into a free trade area, with the economic difficulties created by both Jamaica and Trinidad having well-developed industries.

There were other reasons, too, why the Federation did not last. It was decided that the capital should be in Trinidad—and that did not make the Jamaicans very happy. Then, too, few of the islands' more powerful leaders were prepared to exchange their position for a seat in the Federal parliament. This meant that the Federal team never became strong

42

enough to overcome the self-interest of the individual territories. After the Jamaican decision to secede from the Federation, following Mr. Norman Manley's defeat, all attention was turned to Trinidad. Would she accept the challenge and take on the role of leader of the Federation? If not, there was no hope for it. The answer from Trinidad's chief minister, Dr. Eric Williams, was "No". Trinidad could not support the weaker small islands single-handed; she would withdraw and, like Jamaica, go for her own independence.

It was all a great pity. The idea of a Federation made—and still makes—sense: it is difficult for small islands or groups of islands with only a few thousand population to be independent; and some of the islands of the British West Indies are very small in area and population. Nevis, for example, has an area of 50 square miles (129 square kilometres) and a population of 4,000 people. With St. Kitts and Anguilla—two other members of the Leeward Islands group—they formed one territory within the Federation. Besides having their own local government, the three islands were represented in the Federal Senate. In 1969 Anguilla broke away from St. Kitts and Nevis and declared her independence of her sister islands.

The Federal Senate was one of the two Houses of Representatives which were set up under the Federation, and consisted of nineteen members, nominated by the Governor-General. The second House was the Federal Legislature. Each of the main islands and territories of the Federation elected representatives to the Federal Legislature which had forty-five members. The chief executive of the Federation was called the Prime Minister.

Ever since 1944, the British government had been working towards independence for its West Indies possessions, gradually giving the people more and more power. It was planned that the Governors-General and Governors who had represented the British Crown would be eventually withdrawn, and that, by the end of 1962, the West Indies Federation would be a completely independent dominion within the British Commonwealth of Nations.

Unfortunately, the Federation collapsed. Within a few weeks, instead of being an independent federation of islands with a total population of what would now be over 5,000,000, the British West Indies became more divided than ever before.

Jamaica with its dependencies is now an independent member of the British Commonwealth of Nations. It has a House of Representatives of forty-five members, elected by the people. A leader is chosen by the House of Representatives, and is called the Prime Minister.

As we know, Jamaica is at the northern end of the arc of islands that make up the British West Indies. At the southern end is situated the independent nation of Trinidad and Tobago. In another section we will read about Trinidad and the smaller island of Tobago. Trinidad and Tobago's form of government differs from Jamaica's government. It has a twenty-one-member Senate and a thirty-member House of Representatives.

The leader of the government is also called the Prime Minister. In both Jamaica and Trinidad and Tobago the British Crown is represented by a Governor-General.

In 1966 the island of Barbados also became an independent member of the Commonwealth.

Early in 1967 Antigua, Dominica, Grenada, St. Kitts–Nevis–Anguilla and St. Lucia became West Indies Associate States, adopting a new relationship with Britain under which her powers and responsibilities are limited to matters of defence and external affairs. Similar status was achieved by St. Vincent in 1969. All the remaining islands of the British West Indies have become British dependencies once again.

Now let's learn about the people and how they live.

Jamaica

Jamaicans are proud that their island has the largest area, the largest population, the highest mountains and some of the most beautiful beaches in the West Indies. Jamaica is about two-thirds the size of Wales. The population is over 1,800,000. So Jamaica is important; it contains over half the area and nearly half the population of the British West Indies.

The Blue Mountain range in eastern Jamaica has one peak which is 7,400 feet (2,355 metres) high. There are numerous peaks in the Blue Mountains and other ranges that are over 6,000 feet (1,829 metres) high. The mountains are higher than any others in the Caribbean. There are only 650 square miles (1,046 square kilometres) of flat country on the island.

An open-air market in Jamaica. Note the luscious-looking fruit and vegetables

The north coast of Jamaica is famous for its beaches. These have become popular winter holiday places for thousands of tourists. Many people have bought holiday homes near Montego Bay or Ochos Rios.

Because of its nearness to the United States, which has many industrial and business interests in the island, and the short time it takes to travel from Miami, the American influence is stronger here than in any other "British" island.

We have learned that Columbus discovered this island in 1494, and made a second visit in 1503. At that time, Columbus' ships were caught in a storm, and all but two were lost. These two ships ran ashore on the north coast where those on board were marooned for almost a year.

It was during this period that the Spaniards began to ill-treat the Arawaks who had been helpful and friendly. The Arawaks, in return, refused to provide food, so Columbus and his men had a difficult time until they were rescued and returned to Spain.

Spanish settlement of the big island began in 1509. In 1540, Columbus' family received the whole island as a gift from the king and queen of Spain, as we have already said. The Spanish settlers began to cultivate cotton which the Arawaks had grown only in small quantities. They imported sugar-cane and citrus fruits, also.

Unfortunately, with the worsening in relations between Spaniards and Arawaks, many Indians were captured and forced to do heavy work. Within fifty years, the once great tribe was gone. The Indians had either been killed or died of ill-treatment and disease. It was then that the Spaniards began to bring in Negro slaves from Africa.

1655 saw the beginning of a change of rule on the island;

47

for in that year a group of English soldiers landed near Kingston and marched on Spanish Town.

Most of the Spaniards surrendered without a fight. However, a few soldiers and settlers escaped into the mountains and fought the British for several years. The Spaniards also armed and released many of their slaves who then escaped into the mountains. For many years these slaves fought the British. They attacked sugar estates and small towns.

The Negro fighters came to be called Maroons, from an African word meaning "men who hide in the mountains". It is interesting to know that to this day there is a tiny independent area in the Jamaican mountains called the Land of the Maroons.

The Maroons had their hide-outs in a part of Jamaica called the Cockpit Country. Cockpit is the Jamaican word for what we call a pot-hole. The Cockpit Country is filled with thousands of pot-holes and hundreds of very steep mountain peaks. It is covered with thick jungle and is so wild that in places it has not yet even been mapped.

From their hide-outs in the Cockpit Country, the Maroons attacked the sugar plantations and fought the British Redcoats. There is a part of Jamaica near Montego Bay that is still known as the Land of Look Behind. This name was given to it by the British soldiers who were sent out to fight the Maroons. They learned that the Maroons might attack from any direction. Therefore, when they went out to fight, the soldiers rode two men to a mule. By sitting back to back, one

48

man could be looking forward while the other looked behind.

The Maroons fought the British for more than seventy years. In 1739 a peace treaty was offered; the British guaranteed that the land they occupied would be theirs for ever. They were also promised freedom and independence. The treaty was signed in 1739, and the Maroons have had a titular independence ever since.

When I was in Jamaica, I decided to visit the "King" of the Maroons. The Maroon capital is named Accompong and is a little village of a dozen houses on the edge of the Cockpit Country. There is a "National Assembly" of twenty-six members, elected for five-year terms. The title of the chief executive is Colonel-in-Chief. He too is elected and serves a term of five years.

The Colonel-in-Chief of the Maroons. The people of this tiny state won their independence by waging guerilla warfare against the British for seventy-five years

We have mentioned the Maroons because their history is unusual. Now let's learn about the rest of the people of Jamaica. Most of them are Negroes, descendants of the slaves brought by the Spaniards and British. The white population is in many cases descended from early settlers, estate owners, or even from the buccaneers. In addition, immigrants came from many parts of Europe and the Middle East. We have already learned that many Asians live in the West Indies. There are a number of Indians in Jamaica, and almost 30,000 Chinese.

Whatever their colour, the language of Jamaicans is English, and it is easy to understand a Jamaican when he is in conversation with you. But when some Jamaicans talk to one another it sometimes sounds more like a foreign language. This is because there are many unusual Jamaican expressions and ways of putting sentences together.

If a visitor is leaving, you do not say "Goodbye". You say "Wakgud". This means "Walk good" or "Walk carefully". We might say this is much like our expression, "Mind how you go".

Jamaicans have strange names for birds, animals and insects. Vultures are called "John-crow birds". The starling is called a "kling-kling" bird. Fireflies are known as "peenie-wallies".

We have read about some of the fruits, flowers and crops brought to the West Indies from far-distant lands. In Jamaica, the breadfruit is quite an important food.

Breadfruit trees grow wild on a number of the islands. The fruit is baked, then sliced, just as we would slice a loaf of bread. A common meal for average people is breadfruit with salted codfish. Or often the codfish will be eaten with *ackee*.

The ackee is called a vegetable, although it grows on trees that are sometimes very tall. The tree bears a fleshy orange-red fruit. Inside the fruit there is a yellow part known as the "fingers". These look very much like scrambled eggs. The ackee came to Jamaica from India and is a popular food.

Most Jamaican farmers grow what are called "ground provisions". These are yams, or sweet potatoes, which are also eaten with salted codfish.

Sometimes, when driving along a road in Jamaica, you see signs reading BOMBAY FOR SALE. Bombay is a variety of

Bananas look as if they grow upside-down. At the lower end of the stem is the beautiful red flower of the banana plant

Sugar, bananas and coconuts—three of Jamaica's most important crops—growing in a single plantation

mango—also a native fruit of India—and is considered very good. There are many mangoes, bananas, papaws, pineapples and other fruits grown. This is fortunate, for otherwise the diet of Jamaicans would be very poor. Even with the abundant fruit, the diet of most Jamaicans is not healthy. There are few green vegetables; and most people are too poor to afford fresh meat or fish. One serious need is to teach farmers to grow better and more varied crops.

On this page there is a picture showing three of the most important crops. The tall trees are coconut-palms, also brought to Jamaica by the famous Captain Bligh. On the right-hand side of the picture are banana trees. On the left, and growing between the palms, we can see sugar-cane.

Sugar is still the king of Jamaican crops. Rum is made from sugar, and Jamaican rum is famous. Wherever the land is not too mountainous, there are many large sugar estates. Among other important crops are bananas, citrus fruits, tobacco and Blue Mountain coffee. As we might suppose from the name, this coffee is grown on the mountainsides.

There are two other sources of income for Jamaica which are now almost as important to her as sugar. The first of these is what is called tourism. We have mentioned the beautiful beaches, the lovely mountain scenery. The money spent by tourists, especially those from America, makes this a source of revenue second in importance only to that which comes from sugar.

There are many hotels, especially along the north coast. There are luxurious places which are very expensive, but of course there are also many fine hotels which charge reasonable rates. And the climate gives good holiday weather all year round.

The second important source of income is bauxite, the mineral ore from which aluminium is manufactured. Rich

A bauxite shipping terminal

bauxite deposits have been discovered in Jamaica, and several American companies are now mining it and shipping it to factories in the United States.

Jamaica's important products now rank in this order: sugar, tourism, bauxite, bananas and tobacco.

Now let's pretend that we can take a quick trip over the island to see what it looks like and to learn more about the people. One of our photographs shows a boy with a mule. In the mountains, many people travel on mules.

In the other picture, women are carrying bananas on their heads. All through the West Indies we find that people "use their heads" in this way. This is one African custom that has continued through four centuries; for, in Africa, people have always carried heavy burdens on their heads.

A West Indian boy and his transport. For the mountain people, the mule is one of the most convenient forms of travel

Bananas are picked by the men but the girls "head" them to the waiting trucks for shipment

However, we must not think that Jamaica is a primitive country. In spite of its mountains, Jamaica has a fine road system. It is possible to drive to all parts of the island, even to

Accompong, capital of the Land of Maroons. There are two main railways, connecting Kingston with Montego Bay and Port Antonio.

While there are many very poor people, living in huts scattered through the mountains, there are also modern towns. Kingston, Jamaica's capital, has a population of 400,000. It is the largest city in the British Islands, an important port, and an educational centre. The University College of the West Indies is located in this city. Until this university was opened in 1948, West Indians went to England or Canada for university training.

We have learned that Jamaica was granted a constitution in 1944 and that its citizens have enjoyed self-government for some time. Jamaicans can be proud of the progress they have made, but many problems are still facing them. There is still not enough being done in the way of training and education. Poverty is a serious problem: many people still live in tiny shacks. In addition, very few farmers know about modern methods and they do not use the modern fertilisers that would make the land produce better crops.

Because there is not enough work in Jamaica, a high percentage of the West Indians who arrive in Britain every year have been Jamaicans. Britain, they have been taught from schooldays, is "home", and a place to which they have every right to go for a higher standard of living.

Before we visit the other main islands, let's learn about the smaller islands which were dependencies of Jamaica until that

Inter-island schooners—a typical West Indian harbour scene

island's independence. Now the Caymans and the Turks and Caicos are back to being British dependencies. The Cayman Islands are located 178 miles (286 kilometres) north-west of Jamaica. There are three islands, named Grand Cayman, Cayman Brac and Little Cayman. The largest, Grand Cayman, is 21 miles (34 kilometres) long and 7 miles (11·2 kilometres) wide. The Cayman Islands have a total area of 100 square miles (161 square kilometres) and a population of about 9,000.

Until recently, the people here were mostly white, in many cases descendants of the buccaneers. The famous Captain Henry Morgan once lived on Grand Cayman, and the ruins of his castle can still be seen. Some people maintain that there is buried pirate treasure on this island.

The main industries are boat-building, and fishing for huge sea turtles. The Caymans have beautiful beaches, and tourism has also become very important to them.

To reach the Turks and Caicos Islands, one must sail round or fly over the big island of Hispaniola. These islands are really a part of the Bahamas, and were settled by people from the Bahamas or from Bermuda. The largest island is only $7\frac{1}{2}$ miles (12 kilometres) long. There are several score of tiny uninhabited islands called *cays* (pronounced like "key"). The area of the Turks and Caicos is 166 square miles (430 square kilometres), and the population is over 6,000. Salt is the main product.

The Leeward Islands

It is a long journey (over 700 miles—1,126 kilometres) from Jamaica to the British Leeward Islands, its nearest neighbours in the British group of islands. There are six large islands in the Leewards belonging to the British West Indies. (As we have learned, there are also some French and Dutch islands in this group.) The area of these six islands is about 421 square miles (1,090 square kilometres), and the population is 147,000.

St. Johns is the capital and the largest city. It is in Antigua, pronounced "Anteega". The other inhabited islands are St. Christopher, better known as St. Kitts; Nevis, which is pronounced "Neevis"; Montserrat ("Monserrah"), Anguilla ("Angwillah") and Barbuda.

We have already read in the section on geography that Antigua, Barbuda and Redonda are among the older islands; this means that there are no high mountains on them. The highest point on Antigua is about 1,300 feet (396 metres). St. Kitts, Nevis and Montserrat are among the younger, inner chain of islands; and from a plane it looks as though there were no flat land at all on them. Mt. Misery on St. Kitts is 3,711 feet (1,131 metres) high and appears to occupy the whole island; even tiny Nevis has a mountain 3,596 feet (1,096 metres) high. There is still volcanic action on these islands.

The steep mountains are covered with trees. While there is running water on the heavily forested islands, Antigua, which is flat with low hills, has a serious water problem, and

A view of two islands: St. Kitts is in the foreground; Nevis is seen
across the water. Both islands are volcanic

most of its supply must come from rainfall stored in reservoirs.
Despite this water shortage, Antigua has a surprising variety
in its flora, and its crops are similarly wide-ranging, including
date-palms and pineapple.

We do not have space to make a long visit to each island,
so let's learn one or two important facts about the larger ones.
St. Kitts is often called "The Mother of the Antilles",
because it was here that the English first settled, moving on
from St. Kitts to the other Caribbean islands. St. Kitts was
settled in 1623, three years after the Pilgrim Fathers arrived
in New England. French settlers arrived two years later, and
took the island over from the British.

In 1713, Great Britain again gained control, but in 1782
France became the owner for another year, after which the

60

island was restored to Great Britain. The capital of St. Kitts is Basse-Terre, a French name pronounced "Basstair".

In Montserrat the people speak with a definite Irish accent. It was colonised by Irish settlers in 1632. Plymouth is the main town, and it looks much like an Irish village.

Antigua is the most important and best known of the British Leeward Islands. In olden days sugar was made in mills like the one in our picture. As with our windmills, power was provided by sails driven round by the wind.

At one time, there were mills like this all through the West Indies. Most of them have been destroyed, but on Antigua the mills are still standing—although without their sails— and can be seen on every part of the island. Antiguans are so proud of these ancient mills that a picture of a sugar-mill appears on Antiguan stamps.

Nowadays sugar is made in modern factories: it is Antigua's most important crop. Another important crop on Antigua and on the other Leeward Islands is sea-island cotton, also grown on the Windward Islands. This cotton is unusual because it has very long fibres.

We have read about Lord Nelson and Admiral Rodney,

This building, which looks like a ruined fort, was once a flourishing sugar-mill; one of many on the island of Antigua

the famous naval heroes whose ships sailed from English Harbour. Antigua is especially interesting because of its ancient forts and because of Nelson's Dockyard, which is still standing.

By contrast with the ancient fortifications, there is now an American military base on the island; it is one of those used to track missiles fired from Cape Kennedy in Florida. This means that when a missile is fired, the American servicemen on Antigua keep a record of its course by using special electronic equipment.

As with many of the other islands, Antigua also has beautiful beaches and fine hotels.

Remember some of the unusual names used by Jamaicans to describe birds and insects? In the Leeward Islands also there are names that are unusual. A "fig" tree here is not what we would suppose. It is a variety of a low-growing banana. And if you visited any of the islands, you would hear a noise every night that is produced by something no one

A view of Nelson's Dockyard

ever sees. On all the islands of the Lesser Antilles there are thousands of tiny tree frogs which begin their musical whistle as soon as the sun goes down. No one ever sees the frogs, and some people say they are crickets. The chorus of the little frogs is heard everywhere, although the note may be different from island to island.

The Windward Islands

If we were visiting all the islands of the British West Indies, we would probably travel on planes of the British West Indian Airways. A daily flight in each direction by a plane called the "Island Hopper" links the territories and supplements the larger international services. As we flew over the many islands of the Lesser Antilles, we would see how mixed up their ownership became after the Caribbean wars ended.

After leaving Antigua the plane flies over the large French island of Guadeloupe, a smaller French island named Marie-Galante, then a British island, then another large French island! The British island is Dominica, which is very mountainous. It lies between the two large islands of the French West Indies.

The main islands in the Windward group are Dominica (pronounced "Domineeka"); St. Lucia, which is pronounced "Loosha"; St. Vincent and Grenada, which is pronounced "Grenayda". Between St. Vincent and Grenada there is a chain of small islands called the Grenadines. The area of the Windward Islands is 821 square miles (2,126 square kilometres)

St. Lucia, like other islands in the Windward group, has high mountains, covered with tropical vegetation. The mountain shown here is volcanic

and the population some 350,000. The capital is St. George's located near the southern tip of Grenada.

The Windwards belong to the inner chain of mountainous, volcanic islands. Each island has high mountains, and there are several active volcanoes. The mountains are covered with trees and dense tropical vegetation. Fortunately for the islanders, there is plenty of running water.

By learning some of the names of cities and mountains, we realise that the Windward Islands must have changed hands and that they were once occupied by the French. The capital of Dominica is Roseau; the two highest peaks on this island, both nearly 5,000 feet (1,523 metres) in elevation, are Morne Diablotin and Morne Trois Pitons.

Castries, another French name, is the capital of St. Lucia. This island did not become permanently British until 1814, with the result that most of its inhabitants still speak a mixture of French and English.

The many steep mountains on the Windward Islands make the life of the people somewhat different from that on other islands. There are beautiful beaches but fewer roads and hotels. For these reasons, the tourist business has not developed at the speed that it has elsewhere, although it is now showing signs of a more rapid development.

In Dominica, St. Vincent and on the Grenadines the mountains have made it difficult to build anything more than a moderate-sized airport; in fact, until quite recently travel in and out was restricted to ships or small amphibious planes.

While these islands do produce both sugar-cane and sea-island cotton, they are not grown on such a large scale here as elsewhere: it is very difficult to clear steep mountains for planting. There are, however, some unusual crops which produce a moderate income. St. Vincent is the "arrowroot capital" of the world. An easily digestible starch comes from this plant which is used in babies' food. The largest single importer of arrowroot is the United States.

Grenada calls itself the Spice Island. Nutmeg, cloves, cinnamon and ginger are important crops here. The growing of bananas, cocoa, coconuts and numerous fruits is also important on all the islands.

We have already read that Captain Bligh brought the first

A St. Vincent girl, carrying sea-island cotton

breadfruit trees to the West Indies. The first tree he brought is still growing in the Botanical Garden at Kingston, St. Vincent. This is the oldest botanical garden in the Western Hemisphere.

It is in Dominica and St. Vincent that the last remaining Carib Indians live. There is a large reservation in Dominica, and most of the remaining Caribs are found on that island. It is interesting to know that the Caribs fought so fiercely on Grenada that the British gave up attempts to settle the island. A few years later, the French bought the island for some beads, a few hatchets and knives and two bottles of brandy—much in the same way as the Dutch bought Manhattan before Nieuw Amsterdam became New York.

Barbados

Barbados is an unusual island. With an area of 166 square miles (430 square kilometres), it supports almost 240,000 people. Great Britain is often called crowded, but in the British Isles the population density is lower.

The correct pronunciation is "Barbaydoss", with the accent on the second syllable. The people of Barbados are called Bajans, and most of them speak English, with an accent that has marked West Country characteristics. Bajans call their island "Little England", and have always been very loyal to the British Crown. The island was continuously

A harbour policeman, Barbados. These men are proud of their uniforms which serve as a link with the past

under British rule for 335 years. The people of Little England like to do things in an English manner. For example, the harbour police of Bridgetown, the capital, wear uniforms exactly like those worn by Lord Nelson's sailors almost two hundred years ago.

Barbados has a wonderful climate, beautiful beaches and more hotels for its size than any island in the Caribbean. Even though there are no mountains, and the island is small, Barbados does not share the water problem of some of the other outer islands. The reason for this is that under the island there is a huge lake of pure, fresh water. In some places, the water even bubbles out into the ocean.

Everywhere one travels on the good roads, one sees fields of sugar-cane, for Barbados is one of the world's greatest sugar producers.

The soil is very rich, and only very few of the forests which once covered the island now remain: the rest have been cleared away. There are a few monkeys in the forest tract. The only other animal of any size is the mongoose, which has long since killed all the snakes.

Barbados is unusual, too, in that it was not discovered by

Although Barbados is known as "Little England", this avenue with its graceful lines of palm trees could hardly be mistaken for a British suburban road

Barbados—the view from Hackleton's Cliff, overlooking the Atlantic

Columbus. Perhaps this is because it is the most easterly of the West Indies. It lies far out in the Atlantic and off the course of ships exploring the island chain. It was discovered by Spaniards who named it Los Barbados, "The Bearded". It is probable that this name was given because of beardlike vines growing on the trees.

Sugar-cane was brought to Barbados from Brazil, and at one time there were over one hundred sugar factories on the island. Now there are fewer but more modern factories. In addition to producing sugar, syrup and rum, Barbados grows fine tobacco. It is also famous for its flying fish: over two thousand people are engaged in catching the fish, many of which are canned for markets abroad. Flying fish, not surprisingly, are a local speciality and are served in the hotels.

70

As on many of the other islands in the West Indies, many people cannot afford fresh meat, or even fresh flying fish. Salt codfish, corn and yams are the diet of a large number.

The West Indians are fond of sport. The most popular game among West Indian boys—and, for that matter, adults too—is "cricket, lovely cricket"; it is their enthusiasm which has produced so many good West Indian cricketers. Baseball, the sport of the islands and mainland territories all around, has made no inroads against this traditional British game, and when a Test Match is being played, nearly all business stops. Football is also popular.

Many West Indian boys and girls also love to fly kites. Often the kites are home-made, parts of them being dried sugar-cane blades called "trash bone".

This is a good place for us to learn about going to school

The inner harbour, Bridgetown, Barbados

in the West Indies. One of the problems here is that, while ordinary schooling is free, boys and girls must pay for higher education. However, although many West Indians are too poor to pay, there is a fair scholarship system.

Children study all the subjects studied in English schools, including English history, and the history of the many countries of the British Commonwealth. In most schools, the boys and girls wear uniforms. The girls wear very much the same kind of uniform as in England. Khaki shorts are favoured for the boys, with no jackets, of course.

Like the majority of the houses, the older schools in Barbados and elsewhere are still mostly made of wood.

Better education for everyone is a problem in Barbados, as elsewhere in the West Indies. But we will read more about the many problems facing this whole area after we have visited the last important islands.

Trinidad and Tobago

Trinidad is separated from the mainland of South America by the Gulf of Paria. Two peninsulas, one each end of the island, extend towards the Venezuelan coast to make this gulf into an almost land-locked body of water. As the plane approaches the airport of Port of Spain, it is possible to see the mountains of Venezuela.

We have learned that Columbus discovered Trinidad. The

72

early Spanish explorers gave interesting names to the narrow channels separating Trinidad from Venezuela. The southern channel is called Boca de la Sierpe which means Serpent's Mouth. The northern channel is called Boca del Dragon, meaning Dragon's Mouth. These names were given because of the dangerous tides which sweep through the narrow channels and which caused many shipwrecks.

Trinidad and Tobago have been governed as one since 1889. As we learned, these islands were connected to the South American mainland millions of years ago; therefore the vegetation, animal and bird life is similar to that found in nearby Venezuela.

The northern end of Trinidad is very mountainous and covered with thick jungle. Among the many wild animals, there are monkeys, peccaries, agoutis and a few "tigers" as the South Americans call jaguars. There is also a strange little animal called the armadillo which is covered with scales rather like armour. Among the many tropical birds, there are brightly coloured parrots and humming-birds. When Columbus discovered Trinidad in 1498 it was inhabited by Carib Indians who called the island *Iere*, meaning "Land of the Humming-bird".

Trinidad became the capital island of the short-lived West Indies Federation. Port of Spain, a city of 100,000 people, is the capital of the island. The area of Trinidad is 1,862 square miles (4,944 square kilometres), which is almost exactly the size of Lancashire. The population is about 860,000. Thus we see that Trinidad is second in area and population to Jamaica. It is the richest of the islands, with some unusual products which we shall read about later.

If we were to travel over the island, we would see that it differs from all the other islands. We would discover this in the short drive from Trinidad's big airport at Piarco to Port of Spain. There are rice fields along the road, often being cultivated by farmers with their water-buffaloes. There are many Hindu women dressed in saris, the traditional dress of India. We would see Hindu schools and temples, and Moslem mosques; we might see a Hindu holy man walking along the road. One third or more of the population of Trinidad is Asian. There are over 300,000 people, Hindus and Moslems, from India, and thousands of Chinese too.

Trinidad was occupied by the Spaniards for almost three hundred years. For this reason, we would find many places with Spanish names like San Fernando, the island's second city. At one time, a large number of French families settled on the island too. In fact, there are people of almost every nationality and race living in Trinidad.

Trinidad is famous for several things. It is the home of calypso and of the steel band. Calypso is a type of island folksong set to music with African rhythms. A steel band is a group of musicians who play on sections of oil drums—or on anything made of steel. Each section of steel is hammered, and treated with fire and water, so that it is possible to get many different notes by striking the drum.

74

A small Trinidad steel band

The Trinidad Carnival, which is celebrated on the two days before Ash Wednesday each year, presents a fantastic sight and sound. There are calypsos, steel bands, parades, floats and lavishly-costumed groups, some several hundred strong.

We have said that Trinidad is a rich island. It produces sugar, rum, cocoa, coconuts, citrus fruits and rice. Unlike the other islands, it is fortunate in having rich oil deposits and several large oil refineries. And from Trinidad has come asphalt to pave streets all over the world.

An Indian farmer and his wife. Their cart is drawn by water buffaloes

Let's visit La Brea, the Pitch Lake, from which pitch or asphalt—a tarlike substance—has been taken for three hundred years. This unusual lake was discovered by Sir Walter Raleigh in 1595. He used the asphalt to patch leaks in his ships. Pitch Lake covers 110 acres (45 hectares) and is over 285 feet (87 metres) deep. It has been said to be inexhaustible, but in fact the excavations over the years have lowered the level of pitch quite considerably.

You can walk on the lake, or drive a car on it even, for the surface is quite firm; but if you stand still, your feet will sink in almost without your noticing it—and so will a car's wheels if it is left in one place.

The asphalt is dug either with a pick or with a big scoop-

This machine is digging asphalt

like machine. The machine dumps the asphalt into trucks, and the scoops leave a large hole in the surface of the lake. But within a matter of days the hole is filled with new asphalt that pushes up from below.

In the asphalt are bits of petrified wood, fossils and the bones of animals that lived thousands of years ago. Before it can be marketed, the asphalt is melted and cleaned. Then it is piped into barrels and shipped all over the world.

Some of the people who live in nearby villages have made their own paved walks and front yards. They dig up big pieces of asphalt which are left to melt in the sun and can then be smoothed out by hand.

Trinidad's carnival is gay and colourful. The people dress up specially for the occasion, as in this picture

There is an interesting legend about the Pitch Lake. Many centuries ago, a great battle took place between two Indian tribes. The victorious tribe built a village where the lake is now located, and held a big victory celebration. They killed hundreds of beautiful humming-birds, ate the flesh in the victory feast, and used the feathers to decorate their clothing. The Great Spirit was angered that the beautiful little birds had been killed. As punishment, he caused the entire Indian village to sink into the earth. The hole where the village lies buried has been filled with asphalt ever since!

Now let's visit Tobago (pronounced "Tobaygo"), the little island north-east of Trinidad. Tobago has an area of 116 square miles (300 square kilometres) and a population of more than 40,000. The capital is Scarborough. After changing owner-ship numerous times, Tobago finally became a British posses-sion in 1803, and has been administered as a part of Trinidad since 1889.

You may have read the story of Robinson Crusoe, who was shipwrecked on an uninhabited island. The people of Tobago claim that there really was such a man, and that he was marooned on their island. They will even show you the cave where he was supposed to have hidden. There are other islands, however, which claim that Daniel Defoe got his inspiration from them. Tobago is a beautiful, tropical island, and whether or not it actually happened to Crusoe it would certainly be fun to be shipwrecked there!

Tobago is unusual because it is the only island of any size

This cocoa tree at the agricultural station in Tobago is seven years old

in the West Indies where sugar is no longer produced. Now, coconuts, bananas and cocoa are the important crops. There are several large coconut estates. Let's take a quick visit to a big estate to learn something about coconuts.

Coconuts are not picked. About every two weeks, workers go among the trees collecting up all the nuts that have dropped. These are then taken to the factory where a "cutter" slashes each nut into four pieces. He uses a big knife called a cutlass. Other workers dig out the white "meat" which is taken to a huge oven to be dried. The "milk" is not used for anything—except a wayside drink.

Once dried, the white meat, called copra, is shipped away to be made into oil for use in soap, margarine and for cooking oils. West Indians say the coconut is a fine tree to grow. It begins bearing nuts when it is from five to seven years old. An average tree will live for from fifty to one hundred years. And all that time, regardless of season, it bears.

Tobago has another unusual claim to fame. Many years ago, an English newspaperman named Ingram became interested in the lovely greater bird of paradise, found only on the distant Aru Islands of New Guinea. Hunters were killing the birds for their beautiful plumage, and Ingram realised that this bird—sometimes called the most beautiful in the world—would soon be extinct. He therefore decided to buy Little Tobago, a small island just off Tobago's east coast. Then he arranged for some of the birds to be caught in the jungles of the Aru Islands, and had them shipped half-way across the world to Little Tobago. The first birds arrived

The coconut is one of Tobago's main crops. The man in the left-hand picture is a coconut cutter

This view gives some
idea of the beauty of
Tobago

in 1912, and, within a year or two, forty-five birds were released on the island.

Little Tobago has an area of only 450 acres (182 hectares) and cannot support many of these beautiful birds. It is thought that there are about fifty living and breeding there now. The birds of paradise are protected, and it is possible to hire a boat and guide and visit Little Tobago to see the lovely creatures which have travelled so far from their original home.

Problems of New Nations

We have now visited the most important islands of the British West Indies. We have learned that the islands differ from each other in some ways, while having many similar problems. Jamaica is large in area and population but has much poverty. Trinidad is the richest island, largely because of oil, and it has more and better paying jobs. Barbados is very English, while one-third of Trinidad's population is Asian.

It is not surprising, in the face of this variety of race and circumstance, that there are differences of opinion and jealousies. We get some idea of the sort of problem to be solved when we realise that, for instance, each major island still has its own postal system, with different stamps. There are also different systems of taxation. People still cannot move freely from one island to another. For example, it is very difficult for a Jamaican to go to Trinidad and find employment in an oil refinery. Very few people have ever visited islands other than the one on which they were born. Aeroplane travel is gradually changing this, however, and it is now possible to go from one end of the islands to the other in a day.

As more West Indians travel and become better acquainted with their country, some problems will disappear. People will begin to think as West Indians rather than as Jamaicans or Bajans. But for most, it will be a long time before they can afford such travel.

Serious problems will remain. There are too few educated people; there are not enough jobs for the population, which is increasing rapidly. There are too few factories and sugar is

Housing is sometimes an urgent problem in the West Indian towns.
In the villages it is less urgent since there are many houses like this wooden one. Note the bougainvillea round the door

still too much relied upon economically, with the added disadvantage that other countries now compete with the West Indies by producing more sugar, often at cheaper prices.

New crops are needed. Factories are needed, so that people will not have to depend so much on agriculture. Farmers must learn new methods, so that more and better crops can be produced. The British government is helping the West Indies in several ways, and discussions are taking place to try to find a more satisfactory permanent solution to the problems of this area.

One way in which the West Indies can improve their economic situation is to have more visitors. We have learned that tourism is already an important business. We have read about the beautiful beaches, the fine climate. We know also that most tourists only visit the islands during the winter season. The West Indies governments hope to show that the islands can be visited at any time because the weather is always pleasant.

As the islands gradually loosen their ties with Great Britain, there will, no doubt, be more and more trade with the United States, whose influence in the area has grown in recent years.

Summing up: We know that most of the people in the West Indies are Negroes; but we also know that there are many Hindus, Moslems, Chinese and people of British and Irish descent. Yet there is no segregation, no racial discrimination in the West Indies. Children of all races go to

A rural West Indian school

school together. In the government of Trinidad, there are Negroes, Moslems, Hindus, Chinese and Europeans. This situation reflects the influence of British democratic principles, and is the result of the descendants of African slaves, English estate owners, and indentured workers from India, all working together.

Now we will visit the islands of the French West Indies and the Netherlands West Indies, whose citizens also have self-government, but in a different way.

The French West Indies

France once owned Canada, Louisiana in the U.S.A. and almost all the islands of the West Indies, including the part of Hispaniola called Haiti. Now all that is left of this colonial

84

empire is a few islands. The French West Indies consist of Martinique in the Windward Islands, between Dominica and St. Lucia, and Guadeloupe, which is in the Leeward Islands, between Antigua and Dominica. Five smaller islands are administered from Guadeloupe and are called dependencies. The total area of the French West Indies is 1,138 square miles (2,939 square kilometres), and the population is over 600,000.

The people of these islands are much like those living in the British West Indies. Their ancestry is the same. Most of the population is descended from African slaves. The food is the same. We find the same plants and fruits; the little mongoose is the most common animal. The only difference is that people speak French rather than English. And cars drive on the right, as in France, rather than on the left.

Both Martinique and Guadeloupe were discovered by Columbus in 1493. Columbus landed on Martinique in 1502, but actual settlement did not begin until 1635. Many battles were fought over the possession of the islands. Guadeloupe was taken by the British several times, and came under permanent French rule in 1815. For eighteen months, the English Admiral Hood held Diamond Rock off Martinique. The French attacked the rock many times but could not conquer it. However, the English never conquered the island, and Martinique has been under French control for over three hundred years.

The people of the French islands are just as loyal to France as Bajans are to England. They are French citizens, enjoying

Martinique is a volcanic island. This ruined cathedral is a poignant reminder of that fact

all the rights of people who live in France. Guadeloupe and Martinique are *départements* of France. People elect their local officials, and each of the big islands elects representatives to the French National Assembly.

Martinique has an area of 450 square miles (1,165 square kilometres) and a population of 300,000. It is a volcanic island, very mountainous and covered with tropical vegetation. We have read about the eruption of Mt. Pelée in 1902. Great streams of lava poured down the sides of the mountain into St. Pierre, the capital. Our picture shows the ruins of the cathedral in St. Pierre, which was never rebuilt.

Mt. Pelée still sends up smoke and steam; but as it is now considered safe, many tourists visit St. Pierre to see the ruins. The eruption of the mountain, which killed 30,000 people, made Martinique famous.

After St. Pierre was destroyed, Fort-de-France became the

capital. It is located on a beautiful harbour and is an important port.

The main products of Martinique are sugar, coffee, bananas and pineapples. Neither this island nor Guadeloupe is as well developed as most of the islands of the British West Indies. There are fewer good hotels, and the islands are not visited by so many tourists—perhaps as much as anything else because the Americans prefer the islands where English is spoken also.

One other claim to fame is that Martinique was the birthplace of Marie Joseph Tascher de la Pagerie in 1763. This girl with the very long name became the Empress Josephine, wife of Napoleon of France.

Guadeloupe and its five dependencies cover 688 square miles (1,782 square kilometres), and have a population of about 300,000. Guadeloupe is really two islands separated by a narrow body of water called the Rivière Salée. The two sections are called Grande-Terre and Basse-Terre. The capital is on Basse-Terre, but the largest city is Pointe-à-Pitre which is on Grande-Terre.

Martinique fishing-boats. Notice the huge nets hung up to dry

The Isles des Saintes, Désirade and Marie-Galante are three dependencies of Guadeloupe, located near the big island. The other dependencies are two hundred miles (322 kilometres) north and separated from Guadeloupe by the British Leeward Islands. St. Barthelemy, called St. Barts, once belonged to Sweden. Then, in 1877, King Oscar II of Sweden decided it was foolish for Sweden to own one tiny island, very far away. So he ceded the island to France and gave the citizens most of the royal property. The population is about 2,300.

St. Martin is the other French island. In the section of this book on the Caribbean wars, we learned how this island was peacefully divided by the French and the Dutch in 1648. The population of the French part is about 5,000.

French is, of course, the official language of the French West Indies; but many people, especially on the large islands, use a dialect called Creole. This is mostly French, but includes some African and some English words. Although in some ways less developed than the British islands, the French islands are quite advanced in their education of children. It is interesting to know that 99 per cent of Martinique's children and 80 per cent of Guadeloupe's children go to school.

The Netherlands West Indies

Although usually called the Netherlands or Dutch West Indies, the six Dutch islands in the Caribbean Sea are officially known as the Netherlands Antilles. The islands are in two groups, and are divided into their own "Leeward Islands" and "Windward Islands": the three Dutch Leeward Islands lie close to the coast of South America; and the three Dutch Windward Islands are south-east of Puerto Rico. The total area of the Netherlands Antilles is 394 square miles (1,021 square kilometres) and the population is 204,000.

Let's first read about the Dutch Leeward Islands: Aruba, Bonaire and Curaçao (pronounced Cure-as-sow). These are close to the coast of South America, and differ from all the other West Indies in climate, geography and people.

Rainfall on Aruba is only 17 inches (43 cms) a year; on Curaçao rain averages 22 inches (56 cms) annually. There is no tropical jungle: the most common plants are varieties of cactus and the divi-divi tree. This tree, which produces beans

Because of low rainfall, vegetation on the Dutch Leeward Islands is different from that on other islands of the West Indies, as can be seen from the cacti in this picture

used in tanning leather, grows in all kinds of strange shapes—the result of continuous pressure from the prevailing winds.

Because of the low rainfall, sugar never became important. This fact has meant that there are fewer Negroes, and more people of other races than of African descent, although many West Indians work in the oil refineries there.

Aruba and Curaçao are very rich islands—because of an accident of geography. Near by, on the coast of Venezuela, there is a large, almost land-locked bay called Lake Maracaibo. A sand-bar across the mouth of this bay makes it impossible for big ships to enter. Around the bay is one of the richest oilfields in the world. Since big tankers cannot enter Maracaibo Bay, large oil refineries were built on nearby Aruba and Curaçao. One refinery on Aruba, built by an American company, is the largest in the world. Over fifty ships a day enter the harbour of Willemstadt, capital of the Netherlands Antilles, and the big seaport city of Curaçao.

The oil refineries provide jobs for thousands of people and have made the islands rich. Because of the big American refinery on Aruba, there are over two thousand Americans living there. Many of the people of the islands are descendants of the South American Indians who originally lived there and who intermarried with the early Spanish and Dutch settlers. There are also thousands of people of other nationalities who work in the refineries.

Curaçao is the largest of these islands. It has an area of 173 square miles (448 square kilometres) and a population of

132,000. Aruba has an area of 69 square miles (179 square kilometres) and a population of 60,000. Bonaire covers 112 square miles (290 square kilometres) but has only 6,000 inhabitants. It is called "Flamingo Island" because thousands of these beautiful pink birds nest there.

The islands are fortunate not only in their oil refineries: the tourist business brings in still more income. The climate is pleasant, though dry, and the islands have many fine beaches. Schools here are the best in the West Indies.

The government is so wealthy that it has been able to solve the problem caused by little rainfall. On both Aruba and Curaçao there are factories which distil fresh drinking water from sea water. The resulting water is so pure that minerals must be added to give it a natural "taste".

This Dutch mill was brought from Holland and re-erected on the north-west coast of Aruba

The official language of the Netherlands Antilles is Dutch, but many people on the islands speak both English and Spanish. Among themselves, people speak Papiamento, a mixture of Dutch, Spanish, English and Portuguese. There is also a written form of this language. A sign along a road reading NO TIRA SUSHI AKI means "No Rubbish to be Dumped".

The three Dutch Windward Islands are almost 600 miles (966 kilometres) north-east of the Dutch Leeward Islands. Saba, covering less than 5 square miles (13 square kilometres), is an extinct volcano. St. Eustatius, which is called 'Statia, is about 8 square miles (36 square kilometres) in area. 'Statia's capital is called Orangestad (Orange Town). There is also a volcanic peak, called The Quill, on the island. Saba and 'Statia have a combined population of 2,500.

Sint Maarten is the Dutch half of St. Martin, which has been shared by France and Holland since 1648. It is difficult to realise that these small islands were once considered the most valuable property of the Dutch West Indies Company. 'Statia

A Dutch girl on a narrow street in the capital of St. Eustatius

The Dutch Islands have lovely beaches, and underwater swimming is a popular sport

was called the Golden Rock. As many as two hundred ships crowded its harbours in a day.

During the American Revolution, ships used 'Statia as a base from which they sailed to run the British blockade with supplies for the American colonists. Even though small, Sint Maarten had rich plantations three hundred years ago.

The total population of the three islands is 3,700. Although Dutch is the official language, most people prefer to use English. The Netherlands Antilles are self-governing departments of Holland. Each island has representation, based on size of population, in the Legislature, or *Staten*. The Staten has twenty-two members and meets in Willemstadt. The Queen of the Netherlands is represented by a governor.

The history of the Netherlands Antilles is closely related to the early history of New York. Earlier in this book we read about Peter Stuyvesant, who became governor of the New Netherlands, as the Dutch colony at the mouth of the

Hudson River was then named. Nieuw Amsterdam, as New York was called, was the capital of the colony. Stuyvesant had first been named governor of Curaçao in 1643, and in 1646 became governor of both Curaçao and the New Netherlands.

Now that we have completed our visit to the West Indies, let's review a few interesting facts.

The people of the French and Dutch islands enjoy self-government, as departments of the mother countries. Numerous islands, once parts of different British colonies, have now either achieved independence within the Commonwealth or internal self-government.

We have learned that the people of the West Indies have a history based on the discovery and settlement of the islands by the Spaniards, French, Dutch and British who, in many cases, moved on to explore North America.

There are people in the West Indies who hope that some day all the islands may become federated in a United States of the Caribbean, instead of being separated into parts of three nations. Perhaps that will never happen. Because the islands are so widely separated, it has been difficult for people living on one island to know about those on other islands. However, we know that this is changing, that the aeroplane is bringing people closer together; and, in fact, it is because of modern transportation that it was possible even to think about the British islands becoming federated as one nation.

Index